9/10

JUMP INTO SPORTS

Swimming

By Bob Temple

It's time to head to the pool. There is a swim **meet** today!

Swimming is a great way to get fit.

Swimming is a fun activity. Learning to swim can help you stay safe in the water.

Swimming is an important skill to learn.

There are four main **strokes** that swimmers use. The **front crawl** is the fastest stroke.

This swimmer is using the front crawl stroke.

Swimmers also learn the **backstroke**. They might learn the **breaststroke** and the **butterfly**, too.

Some swimmers wear **goggles** so they can see underwater.

Swimmers practice the strokes a lot. They also practice breathing as they swim.

For some strokes, the swimmer's face is in the water.

Some people compete on a swim team. At swim meets, they wear **sleek** swimsuits. Some wear swim caps.

Kicking their legs quickly helps swimmers move through the water.

At a swim meet, swimmers race against each other in the different strokes. They compete in races of different lengths, too.

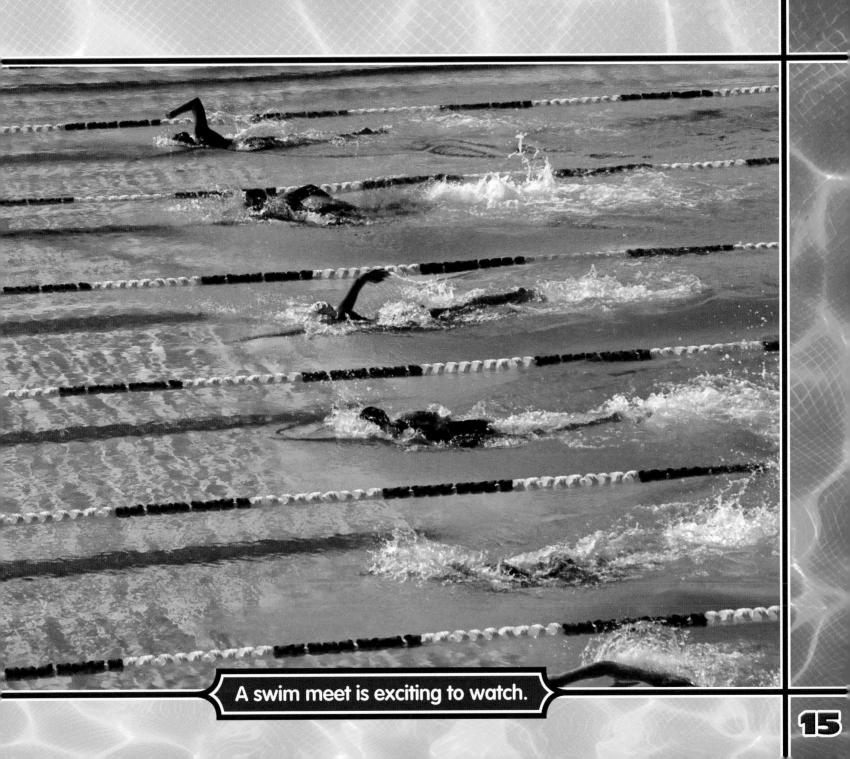

A swim meet is exciting to watch.

To start most races, swimmers get up on the **blocks**. When the starter gives the signal, the swimmers dive into the water. They swim as quickly as they can.

The swimmers have to be careful not to dive before the signal.

Some races are just one or two lengths of the pool. Other races can go for a long time.

In a race, each swimmer has to stay in his or her own lane.

The first swimmer to touch the pool wall at the end of the race is the winner!

Swimmers train hard so they can win at meets.

Glossary

backstroke (BAK-stroke): In the backstroke, the swimmer is on his back and rotates his arms to pull himself through the water. At the start of a backstroke race the swimmers are in the water instead of on the blocks.

blocks (BLOKS): The blocks are the platforms at the end of the pool. Swimmers line up on the blocks to start the race.

breaststroke (BREST-stroke): In the breaststroke, the swimmer is face-down in the water and moves her arms out from her chest and kicks like a frog. The breaststroke can be done for long distances.

butterfly (BUHT-ur-flye): In the butterfly, the swimmer is face-down in the water. The swimmer kicks his legs up and down and moves his arms in a circle to do the butterfly stroke.

front crawl (FRUHNT KRAWL): In the front crawl, the swimmer is face-down in the water and kicks while her arms go in a circle. The front crawl is the fastest swimming stroke.

goggles (GOG-ullz): Goggles are tight glasses that fit around a swimmer's eyes. Goggles help swimmers see underwater.

meet (MEET): A meet is an event where athletes compete. A swim meet is made up of many races.

sleek (SLEEK): If something is sleek, it is smooth. Swimmers wear sleek swimsuits.

strokes (STROHKS): Strokes are methods of swimming. Swimmers learn different strokes to compete in meets.

To Find Out More

Books

Boudreau, Helene. *Swimming Science*. New York: Crabtree Publishing, 2009.

Mason, Paul. *How to Improve at Swimming*. New York: Crabtree Publishing, 2008.

Miller, Amanda. *Let's Talk Swimming*. New York: Scholastic, 2008.

United States Olympic Committee. *Swimming Reader*. Santa Ana, CA: Griffin Publishing, 2004.

Web Sites

Visit our Web site for links about swimming: *childsworld.com/links*

Note to Parents, Teachers, and Librarians: We routinely verify our Web links to make sure they are safe and active sites. So encourage your readers to check them out!

Index

About the Author

In his long writing career, **Bob Temple** has been a sportswriter and an award-winning author. He has written dozens of books for young readers. Bob owns a development house that specializes in creating children's educational books. He lives with his family in Minnesota.

On the cover: Many swimmers wear swim caps and goggles.

Published by The Child's World®
1980 Lookout Drive • Mankato, MN 56003-1705
800-599-READ • www.childsworld.com

ACKNOWLEDGMENTS
The Child's World®: Mary Berendes, Publishing Director
The Design Lab: Design and production
Red Line Editorial: Editorial direction

PHOTO CREDITS: Christine Gonsalves/iStockphoto, cover; Marcus Lindström/iStockphoto, cover; Justin McGowan/iStockphoto, 3; Big Stock Photo, 5, 7, 19; Schmid Christophe/Shutterstock Images, 9; Stana/Shutterstock Images, 11; 123RF, 13; Chad McDermott/123RF, 15; Gert Johannes Jacobus Vrey/Shutterstock Images, 17; PhotoDisc, 20; iStockphoto, 21

Printed in the United States of America in Mankato, Minnesota.
November 2009
F11460

LIBRARY OF CONGRESS CATALOGING-IN-PUBLICATION DATA
Temple, Bob.
  Swimming / by Bob Temple.
     p. cm. — (Jump into sports)
  Includes index.
  ISBN 978-1-60253-373-8 (library bound : alk. paper)
  1. Swimming—Juvenile literature. I. Title. II. Series.
  GV837.6.T46 2010
  797.2'1—dc22   2009030731